Bravo For Bravo

First Dog to Winter Over at the South Pole

by

Sarah Tuck Gillens

Foreword by

Kathleen Tuck Fontaine

Shire Books

Manchester, Vermont

BRAVO FOR BRAVO
First Dog to Winter Over at the South Pole

ISBN Number:
978-1-60571-182-9

4869 Main Street
P.O. Box 2200
Manchester Center, VT 05255
www.northshire.com

NORTHSHIRE BOOKSTORE

Building Community, One Book at a Time
This book was printed at the Northshire Bookstore, a family-owned, independent bookstore in Manchester Ctr., Vermont, since 1976. We are committed to excellence in bookselling. The Northshire Bookstore's mission is to serve as a resource for information, ideas, and entertainment while honoring the needs of customers, staff, and community.

Printed in the United States of America

This book is dedicated to the first crew to winter over at the South Pole:

John Tuck Jr. Lt. (jg), Military Leader

Dr. Paul A. Siple, Scientific Leader

Robert F. Benson, Seismology

Edwin C. Flowers, Meteorology

John F. Guerrero, Meteorology

Herbert L. Hansen, Meteorology

William S. Hough, Ionosphere

William F. Johnson, Meteorology

Arlo U. Landolt, Aurora

Edward W. Remington, Glaciology

Clifford R. Dickey Jr, Electronics

Melvin C. Havener, Mechanic

Earl F. Johnson, Utilities

William C. McPherson Jr, Radioman

Thomas M. Osborne, Builder

Chester W. Segers, Cook

Dr. Howard C. Taylor III, Medical Officer

Kenneth L. Waldron, Electrician

Of course the station would not have been built without the can-do attitude of Richard A. Bowers, Lt. (jg) and his team of Seabees. The supplies, mail and personnel were carried safely by awesome pilots, like Lt. Comdr. Conrad S. Shinn and Lt. Comdr. Roy E. Curtis.

Table of Contents:

Foreword by Kathleen Tuck Fontaine

Storytelling is as old as time, and as important as the subjects it shares. The desire to learn is a worthy characteristic. Then to share within a story what you've learned, to bring it to life, takes passion, and is a gift and skill. By researching information about the South Pole and the explorations occurring there as well as the life of a particular dog, the author, Sarah Tuck Gillens, does just that. In the course of her research, the author found she was related to one of the principal characters you'll meet in these pages; Lt. (jg) John (Jack) Tuck, Jr., my father.

In addition to being a geographer, Jack Tuck was an educator, in and out of the classroom. He felt it was important for children and adults alike to question, to seek answers. He never lost his patience with me after the countless, repetitive "But why Daddy?" questions I'd ask. Asking brought answers and knowledge. The work the men did during Operation Deep Freeze at the South Pole answered questions about seismology, glaciology and the atmosphere and raised even more, and yet many have never heard of any of their research. My father felt it was of great importance for children to study the sciences, in particular geography. He, even in adulthood, questioned and sought answers. Veteran explorer, Paul Siple, also a geographer, and my father worked to carry out the scientific studies at the pole. Paul was his mentor, confidant, and dear friend. When Jack assumed responsibilities as military leader in his early twenties,

Paul was the fatherly figure he could turn to for trusted advice. They spent many hours working beside each other gathering the data that would be shared with the world, and many more hours in conversation over the Scrabble board. Their lives and our families remained entwined even after their return to the States when "Uncle Paul", as we fondly knew him, became my brother's godfather.

I grew up listening to the stories of my father's "time on the ice", the people he worked with, the situations they endured, and the amusing anecdotes, many of which related to the dogs he worked with at McMurdo. Bravo was born there, after they were settled in Antarctica. He was born on August 14, 1956 – the day before my father's 24th birthday. Were it not for the timing alone that made him "Jack's dog"; it was the kinship and fierce bond they shared that made it so. Though Bravo made short work of chewing through some of his heavy woolen socks and attempted to destroy a couple treasured books, he was a perfect companion, bringing humor and friendship into a stark environment. We were always told that as much as Bravo was "Jack's dog", my father was "Bravo's human"! Paul Siple played a significant role in our lives, but I think never more so than in his determined assistance in getting Bravo honorably discharged from the Navy so he could be reunited with my father after they'd returned to the States. Having also worked and bonded with dogs during his previous trips to the Antarctic, Paul knew the importance of their relationship.

What is so wonderfully portrayed in the coming chapters is Bravo's story, linked as it will always be with the men who were his companions. Bravo was there when history was made, when men gathered scientific data that would help nations further their research was gathered, and when friendships were forged that would remain as years passed. This is a story that should inspire one to seek answers, to dive headfirst into learning about our earth sciences, to take the first step on an exploration that could change one's life. Here within these pages one finds a glimpse of the world Bravo saw and experienced…and the author's words encourages one to be just as curious and brave.

Kathleen Tuck Fontaine

"Dogs are not our whole life, but they make our lives whole." — Roger Caras

Pups born at McMurdo. Photo by John Tuck Jr. Courtesy of Dartmouth College Rauner Special Collections Library

Bravo For Bravo

Chapter 1   Bravo wants to go with Jack

In 1956, I was an orphan pup. One morning I woke up six feet from the floor, cradled in the warm hands and silky beard of a tall man. His name was John Tuck Jr., a Naval Seabee officer. His nickname was Jack and I am Bravo. I was born at McMurdo Station in the

Antarctic. Jack's job was to care for thirty sled dogs. I thought my job was to follow Jack around and keep him company.

"How's that pup of ours?" asked Dutch Dolleman, an experienced dog trainer who was cutting up seal meat for the dogs.

"Bravo is growing bigger every day. He watches everything as if he knows that something important is going to happen," Jack replied, setting me down in the dog pen. Jack's hands smelled like leather because he and Dutch had been making sled dog harnesses.

I ran to the other sled dogs and they sniffed me all over. They said that Dutch knew a lot about dogs and about surviving in cold climates. He'd been involved in a rescue of a flight crew in Greenland during World War II.

The dogs had heard the men talking about settlements that would be built around Antarctica as the International Geophysical Year or IGY was starting. This project was called Operation Deep Freeze by the U.S. Navy.

Scientists would come from all over the world to study the climate, the environment and atmosphere. The sun was going to have very strong magnetic storms and sunspots. The men would be observing a magnificent sight of colorful waves of light in the night skies called aurora australis. The ozone layer would be studied and weather balloons would be sent up to study the atmosphere. The thickness of Antarctica's ice would be determined. In other words Antarctica would be examined from top to bottom.

My cousins and I have done our own studies of the environment. We are penned at a dog hut called Dogheim. We've sniffed the frosty air and smelled penguins, lots of them! Our puppy claws dug the hard packed ice and have found more ice. We've watched the night sky come alive with shooting, waving colors and this made our hair stand on end. Sometimes the whole pack of dogs has howled at the moon and it created quite a stir if the men happened to be around.

Jack and Dick Prescott harnessing dogs. Courtesy of the National Science Foundation.

During the day we watched the dogs get harnessed and lined up to pull a sled. They were usually an energetic, noisy bunch of canines! Kao, from Montreal, was a strong lead dog. Towak was my father and was a huge dog. He would tower over the men if he stood with his paws on their shoulders.

Photo of Jack exercising dogs at McMurdo.   Courtesy of the National Science Foundation.

The harnessed dogs pulled a sled across the ice with Jack running along giving commands. He and Dutch worked the dogs every day. Otherwise the dogs are tied up all the time.

"What's your job going to be when you are done raising us?" I asked my aunt as I burrowed into her thick fur with my cousins.

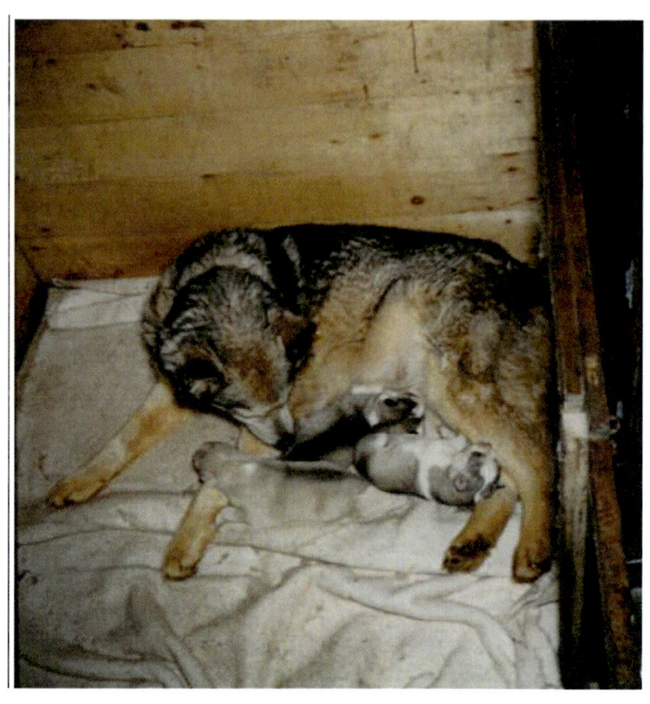

Photo by Jack Tuck. Courtesy of Dartmouth College's Rauner Special Collections Library.

"The dogs are here to help with rescues," Aunt explained. "If any of the planes have to make an emergency landing and can't get back to McMurdo, then drivers, dogs and sleds will be dropped by parachutes for a rescue operation."

"Yikes! I'm glad we're not sled dogs yet!" I yelped to my cousin after I playfully bit his ear.

"Can you imagine being dropped out of one of those planes?"

Cousin wasn't listening. He was rolled up in a tight ball and was asleep with his nose tucked under his tail. I wandered outside and listened to Jack and Dutch. Jack was telling Dutch that he had graduated from Dartmouth College and then went to Greenland to study reindeer. When he heard about this opportunity in Antarctica, he wanted the Navy to give him an assignment.

At McMurdo Jack worked with other Seabees, and they were gathered around Dick Bowers, the building leader for the South Pole station. I loved listening to the men and their plans for the pole.

"No one has attempted this before," Dick was warning the guys about the dangerous, difficult adventure ahead. "The South Pole is about 850 miles inland from here and 9200 feet above sea level. We'll be flown in by ski planes and our supplies will be dropped from the air. October is the start of summer so we can expect temperatures to rise to around zero degrees. We will have some blizzards but the sun will be visible until March," Dick lectured while stamping his feet to keep them warm.

"Which building will be erected first?" asked Jack.

"We'll build a Quonset hut with a heater and cook stove. Some men may sleep in tents and some will be able to sleep in the hut," Dick answered. "We'll use the bulldozer to even out the ice and snow for the bases for all the other buildings, if the bulldozer gets dropped safely. The dogs will have to burrow down into the snow. Jack, you'll make sure they have enough food supplies.

Heater and cook stove sounded good to my puppy ears. I wasn't sure about bulldozers falling from the sky. That sounded scary to me! The sled dogs taught us survival skills such as digging into the snow to keep warm in a blizzard. I was hoping these men also knew how to dig in and stay warm!

The time of departure for the Pole arrived along with bad weather. After several days of frantic activity, the men and equipment settled down like the new fallen snow. Piles of bags were everywhere and the sled dogs were snoozing.

"I can't understand why they aren't more excited," I yipped as I paced at the side of the pen, pleading to go. I wanted to be with all the guys, Jack, Bowers, Bristol, Woody, Montgomery, Nolen, Randall and Powell.

No one had lived at the Pole. It was called an awful place by Robert Falcon Scott in 1912 when he had arrived there with four companions. Besides laboring against strong winds and cold weather, Scott found he had been defeated. The race to the South Pole had been won by Roald Amundsen who had arrived a month earlier. In 1929 Admiral Byrd flew a plane over the South Pole but never landed there.

On October 31, Rear Admiral Dufek, Lt. Comdr. Conrad S. Shinn, pilot, and Capt. William M. Hawkes, copilot, landed the Que Sera Sera at the South Pole. Also with the plane was a crew chief, Petty Officer 2/c John P. Strider; an observer Capt. Douglas L. Cordiner; a navigator, Lt. John Swadener; and Petty Officer 2/c William A. Cumbie Jr., radioman. When they landed, the Pole temperature was 58 degrees below zero.

In the short time it took for the U.S. flag to be raised and photos to be taken, the skis of the plane froze to the icy snow. Fifteen JATO (jet assisted take-off) rockets were fired to get the plane back into the air. Admiral Dufek decided it was too cold at the Pole and the building project was delayed until the 19th of November.

Brave men were going to build enough places to live for the winter and carry out science projects like movements of the glaciers, gravity experiments, seismology studies, the airglow and auroras, geomagnetism, ionosphere physics and cosmic rays. I don't know what any of those things are. I'm just repeating what I heard.

I think men enjoy pushing themselves to do something challenging! Our doggie brains can smell fear. I sensed that these brave men were anxious but they were also strong and smart. I loved to watch them work together, joking with each other at the same time as they got a lot done. I wanted to be part of the fun and work. I wanted to be with Jack!

Chapter 2   Off to the Pole

Pen and ink drawing by Sarah Tuck Gillens.

On November 19, 1956, Jack, Lt. Bowers and his crew of builders loaded two ski planes for the trip to the Pole. On board were eleven sled dogs. Big Globemaster planes flew along to help in locating the Pole and to drop the dog food, sleds, harnesses and heavy equipment down onto the snow. I thought my heart would break when Jack climbed into the plane and disappeared. I ran in circles in the pen until Old Dutch came over and held me tightly against his big jacket.

"He'll be back. He'll be OK," Dutch kept telling me.

Later that day, the radioman reported to Dutch that it was twenty-nine degrees below zero at the Pole, the men were in tents and the dogs were sleeping outside. I heard about supplies that were streaming down to the snow. That meant that the parachute ropes were breaking and goods were free falling to the snow surface. One bulldozer buried itself thirty feet in the snow. Other parachutes would land and sail away across the snow because high winds would fill the chutes. The men had to chase them down. I love to chase things but the men were getting tired and wanted to solve the problem.

Seven days had gone by and I was waiting for news of Jack. Paul came to visit with Dutch and told him that U.S. mail was delivered at the South Pole for the first time. Dr. Siple was a big man. I always sat and behaved myself when he was around. He was definitely an alpha male or leader. Paul informed Dutch that Admiral Dufek wanted Jack to be the Navy officer in charge at the Pole. Dutch chewed on that thought for a minute like a dog gnawed on a bone.

"You're mighty lucky," he told Siple. "Jack's a good boy, as fine as they come. And another thing, this pup you've been eyeing as a mascot, should go to the new station. He's really Jack's dog, and Jack will insist on having him."

Jack came back to McMurdo to work out a solution for the wrecked supplies. I leaped into the air, twisting and turning because I was so glad to see him! Jack let me roam around and he played tug of war with me. I watched him tie supplies onto wooden pallets and wrap them in canvas. Hopefully these pallets would drop safely to the snow surface. Delicate scientific equipment would be flown in by ski planes along with nine scientists led by Dr. Paul Siple.

The next day, Dutch was flapping Jack on the back with his huge mitten.

"I just heard that Admiral Dufek has appointed you as the Navy support officer in charge at the Pole this winter. There will be long, dark days in that awful cold. What are you going to do for entertainment?" Dutch said, smiling at Jack but winking at me.

"I know what you mean, Dutch. We've seen most of the movies by now. The men like to read and we plan to give lectures." Jack turned and looked at me. I sat very still but I couldn't keep my tail from wagging vigorously.

"What do you say, Bravo? Do you want to spend the winter with eighteen guys and a lot of cold weather?" Jack asked, as he hugged me. I licked his bearded face and howled in delight. Then we packed up my bed and dish. To be with Jack was all I needed and I knew we were off on a great adventure.

Chapter 3   Arrival at the Pole

Que Sera Sera with skis, first plane to land at the South Pole.
Courtesy of the National Science Foundation

I was on a U.S. Navy, ski-equipped, R4D plane with Jack and we were heading to the South Pole Station. My ears were making weird popping sounds and my stomach felt funny. Jack didn't give me any food or water. I was grumpy! Everything looked white below us. Without smelling the air, how did we know where we were going? We had to trust the pilot. I hoped that Jack wasn't going to drop me from the sky, hitched to a parachute as my mom had described when talking about the dog sled rescue drill.

Jack had come back to McMurdo Station to get his gear together after he accepted the Officer in Charge job. I didn't have much gear, just my chain and food bowl. At McMurdo, the dogs had eaten dog food and seal meat. I'd gladly give up seal meat for whatever the guys were eating. I don't suppose I'd be seeing any more penguins. I was going to miss those little guys who studied the activities at McMurdo as if they were building inspectors. They would stand around in their black and white suit-like feathers and discuss what they saw happening.

"Penguins are very smart," Doc Siple told Jack and Dutch at Dogheim. "When I was here, as a Boy Scout with Admiral Byrd's first expedition, one of my jobs was to capture some penguins. Scientists wanted to study them. I rounded up Emperor and Adelie penguins and put them in a deep pit. I fed them and left for the night. The next day they were gone. The penguins had chiseled a stairway out of the ice, up the side of the pit, with their beaks. They had climbed the stairs and disappeared. The next group of penguins was lowered into a pit with a picket fence around the top made from bamboo rods. This group found freedom by pecking out the steps and then loosening enough poles to escape."

"The last pit was edged with heavy oil barrels, too big for the penguins to move. The new group of birds studied the pit. I would sneak over and hear the penguins discussing plans and hear them chipping a stairway but when I looked over the barrels, one penguin would signal the others to stop and they would totter around innocently while I watched them. Later in the day, I was surprised to see penguins popping up and over the barrels. When I ran over to the pit, I saw the tallest Emperor penguin standing on the top step. The others were zooming up the ramp onto the tall bird's back and flying over the barrels. I had watched them hatch a plan, work on the stairs and then figure out how to get over the barrels by working together. That's when I concluded that they were very smart birds and that they deserved their freedom!"

"I could have solved the escape problem," Bravo thought. "I would have staked a team of sled dogs around the top of the pit. I doubt the penguins would have messed with those hungry dogs!"

"Ho hum, are we there yet?" I wondered as the plane seemed to drone on forever. I nestled into the coat that Jack let me use for a bed. Now Jack was telling the pilot, Gus Shinn, about his assignment as sled dog caretaker. In 1955 the Navy had sent Dave Baker, Tom McEvoy and Jack to New Hampshire in order to learn how to drive sled dogs and perform rescue procedures.

"Dutch Dolleman, who had been with Admiral Byrd's expedition in 1938, was already at the Chinook Kennels in Wonalancet. Dogs were being delivered from Canada, New England and as far away as Georgia and Wisconsin. We had to work with thirty dogs and have the dogs ready to go to Antarctica in October," Jack was recalling.

"How much time did you have to get this done?" Gus asked.

"Not much time at all. It was already late summer. We had to learn how to fix dog harnesses and repair sleds.

"How did you drive the dogs? There wasn't any snow there," the pilot asked loudly from his seat.

Jack chuckled. "The dogs were driven along country roads using an old Jeep frame instead of a sled. The local people got quite a kick out of us running beside our dogs or riding in that old Jeep."

"Did you live at the kennels?"

"No, we stayed at the Tamworth Inn on twelve dollars a week pay and worked out of the Chinook Kennels." Jack told the men as he moved his tall body to get more comfortable. "We were one week away from sailing for Antarctica when the Navy sent us to parachute jumping school in New Jersey. Dave, Tom and I had a lot to learn in one week. Besides jumping, it was important to know how to land. The parachute had to be gathered up quickly before it had a chance to pull us over miles of frozen ice," Jack concluded.

"Good grief!" my dog brain worried. "How was a rescue dog going to cut the lines or flatten a parachute? Good luck catching a sled on runners as the polar wind takes off with its parachute." I burrowed more deeply into my bed not wanting to think about these problems. I trusted Jack, who continued with his story about getting the dogs to the Antarctic and McMurdo Station. I was snoozing with one ear open.

"Eleven dogs had traveled to Antarctica on the Navy ship named the Edisto with David Baker and me. The other dogs sailed on the USS Wyandot. It took fifty days to sail to McMurdo Station in Antarctica. The ship sailed through the Panama Canal and on to New Zealand. A big storm caused havoc after crossing the equator. The ship was tipping fifty-five degrees and the dogs had to jam themselves between packing crates to keep from sliding back and forth on the deck where they were tied."

"The dogs must have been happy to get off the ship when you stopped at New Zealand," Gus stated.

Jack shook his head. "Actually the New Zealanders were very cautious about rabies. Had the dogs been unloaded, each dog would have been hitched to two men with chains. Another man was to be present with a loaded gun in case any dog got loose. Needless to say, the dogs were left on the ship."

"When the icy waters of Antarctica were reached, the dogs seemed to get excited. Maybe they sensed their trip was almost over. When the ship was unloaded, weasels, snow-cat like vehicles, and a D-2 Caterpillar tractor were used to pull sled

loads of supplies. Dog food was one of the
first loads to be delivered to McMurdo
where the men had already put up a mess
hall tent, a radio tent and tents for the men.

McMurdo Station, January 1957 – US Navy Official photo.
Courtesy of the National Science Foundation.

We would climb up Observation Hill on weekends and could see the station grow. Quonset huts were built for the men. Dogheim was a wooden hut with a canvas cover. It was very cold but the dogs didn't seem to mind as long as they ate well and had shelter from the wind. Dogheim is where Bravo was born and I guess that makes him an Antarctic native!"

"Gee, maybe I'll get a road named after me, if you could call those gritty trails roads," I moaned, as I tried to stretch out my growing legs which were squashed by duffle bags.

The plane's engines sounded different and I stood up and stretched. The men were gazing out of the windows and I could feel excitement in the air. Gus, our pilot had already flown to the Pole with Admiral Dufek. It had been sixty degrees below zero that day. Gus had used a lot of JATO tanks, which act like rockets under the plane. Because the skis had frozen to the ice in the short time the plane had sat there, the boosters helped the plane get off the snow and into the thin air at the Pole

I was anxious to get out of the plane and scared at the same time. The ski plane landed on a strip of snow that had been flattened by a weasel. Jack said that the men had worked hard to scrape out a runway in the snow. He lifted me from the plane.

"Welcome back Jack! Good to see you Bravo!" Dr. Siple said, greeting us with a big smile and a frosty white beard.

"Yikes! This place is a frozen surface for as far as I can see and I can't smell anything, not the ocean, not the penguins. Where am I?" I asked myself as I stood with my tail between my legs.

Chapter 4   Bravo's Introduction to the Pole

Saturday, December 29, 1956

"Jack! How was the flight?" Paul Siple had asked reaching out a mitten-clad paw to pat me. I was dancing around because I was excited to be there. When I was done sniffing around, I looked for Jack, who was heading for a Jamesway hut. I trotted over to him as he turned to make sure that I was coming.

"I bet you're hungry, Bravo. Let's find some chow," Jack said as he snapped my leash to my collar. The hut smelled like hot bread and other warm things. I would learn about these foods once the guys started to share their leftovers with me.

"Leftovers from eighteen plates several times each day," I counted in my head. "I think I'm in heaven!"

That is a bright color lining the walls of your bedroom!" Jack exclaimed when he was being shown around by Paul.

"Doesn't it brighten up my six by eight foot space?" Dr. Siple chuckled as he explained that he had hung a yellowish orange parachute over the insulation in the hut's walls. "It will be an extra barrier to keep out the cold."

Jack's room was across the hall. I sniffed around to make sure it wasn't another dog's territory. Jack hauled his duffle bag in and then we went to find some chow. The cook, Chet Segers, was serving up breakfast foods to the new arrivals. I was given a bowl of scrambled eggs and toast and it was yummy!

Most men were out by the plane unloading equipment. They had to work fast because the pilot kept the plane's engines running so that they wouldn't freeze.

Chet Segers taking bread out of the oven, photo by Cliff Dickey.   Courtesy of the National Science Foundation.

"Jack, come and make the rounds with me," said Dick Bowers after we had eaten. "I'll show you what needs to be done before the long winter. Your crew will have to finish the insides of the structures after we leave."

We went outside into a flurry of activities. Pallets of construction materials were being moved on big sledges pulled by a weasel belching out diesel smoke.

Photo by Dick Prescott. Tracked weasel vehicle used to pull loads. Framing for the station in the background. Courtesy of the National Science Foundation.

The plane had left. I stuck to Jack like frost on a window because so much was going on in all directions. There was a big tower being built. I wondered what its use would be. We walked around and came to an opening in the snow where blocks of hard packed snow were piled. I cocked my head, trying to hear a far off sound. It sounded like a large animal huffing and puffing. I hid behind Jack's tall legs and Jack started to laugh at me.

Entrance to one of the snow mines, Cliff Dickey photo.
Courtesy of the National Science Foundation.

"What's the matter Bravo?" Jack said soothingly as he gently brought me over to the edge of the hole. It looked like a ramp leading down into the cold snow. Soon Dr. Siple emerged from the depths, lugging blocks of snow that he had cut. His face was covered with frost.

"How far are you going with that tunnel?" Jack inquired of Paul who was trying to catch his breath.

"A thousand feet should keep the seismology instruments from picking up vibrations or static from our generators. I've studied the average temperature about six feet down in the snow. It is minus fifty-four degrees. At twelve feet down, the thermometer reads minus sixty-two degrees. This means that we can expect the temperature to drop to minus one hundred degrees this winter. Besides the other uses for the tunnel, I'm going to hide some oranges in it. That will be a nice surprise for the men as a treat this winter!"

Jack admired Dr. Siple's knowledge about cold weather. Paul Siple had studied cold and wind effects. His study produced the Siple Index, later known as the wind chill factor. Dr Siple worked for the Army, being an advisor on cold weather survival in World War II. Jack knew that he was going to learn a lot about cold climates while working with this man who had spent more time in Antarctica than anyone.

Jack and Paul turned towards the buildings that were being constructed as Paul told what an amazing job the Seabees had done while building with a limited number of tools.

"The main tool chest took a dive into the polar snow when its parachute ropes broke," Paul was telling Jack. "The tools were never found. The men had to use spare tools."

"Dick Bowers followed my suggestion that all roofs of the buildings be at the same level. This winter the snow will blow right over us instead of forming snow drifts. The outer hallway around the outside is a necessity in case we need to fight a fire," Paul continued.

Paul kept up his description of the hard working Seabees. "Charlie Bevilacqua, from New Hampshire, and his team are efficient and strong. They're able to build the shell of a building in a day.

Seabees surveying for base of a new building at the pole, Cliff Dickey photo. Courtesy of the National Science Foundation.

"Whoa! Wait a minute.! My finger is bleeding. I didn't know I hit it with the hammer until I saw all this blood," griped Charlie to his gang of builders.

"This finger must be frozen. The rest of you should check for frostbite while I get my finger wrapped up. Keep working so we can finish this building by supper time," Charlie ordered as he headed for the sick bay and Doctor Howard Taylor.

Charles Bevilacqua, Dick Prescott photo. Courtesy of the National Science Foundation.

"I've been picking up the waste materials. We recycle cardboard, turning it into extra insulation," Paul continued as he stomped on a piece of cardboard flying by in the wind. I had already grabbed some cardboard and was shredding it to show the men what great teeth I had!

"See that Seabee? His name is Randall," Paul said pointing to a lean, young man. "He came from a large family in Massachusetts and knows how to eat.

I watched him finish off four steaks one day after working out in the cold. It's important that these men get enough calories to keep warm and to keep moving in this cold climate."

"Eating four steaks is every dog's dream! I liked this conversation," I thought as I searched for a piece of insulation to sit on. I gazed around and saw no "Dogheim" hut. The sled dogs were tethered to a chain and they looked mighty cold. They would be flown back to McMurdo soon. I hope that chain goes with them because I did not want to be tied to it!

Photo by Jim Rooney. Courtesy of the National Science Foundation.

Jack spent most of the day outside. Day is a confusing word as the sun doesn't set from September until March. The men wore sunglasses, plastic ones that did not freeze to their noses. I looked at their eyes and saw myself looking back. I could tell by a worker's voice if he wanted to play with me. Most men were so busy that they didn't see me standing behind Jack.

At lunch time, the most awful sound blasted through the hut where we ate. I jumped up from the floor and started to growl and bark. My hair stood on end, making me look bigger in case I had to fight. I was in battle mode. Everyone scurried out and they were looking everywhere. I knew the sound was coming from some gadget high up on the wall. Ken Waldron hurried in and took the box apart and pulled a wire. Other men were coming in, shaking their heads and saying "no fire." That's when a discussion started about how to prevent false alarms from going off.

The trigger temperature was 135 degrees and sometimes the heat by the ceiling was that hot when the furnace was working hard. Where I bedded down, the floor temperature was a comfortable thirty-two degrees. Doc Taylor came up with a plan to build a control box and Ken Waldron, our electrician, changed all the alarm settings.

Ken Waldron, electrician, Cliff Dickey Photo.
Courtesy of the National Science Foundation

A lot of the guys had trouble sleeping. One would think that the hard labor would exhaust them. The constant light had something to do with the sleep problems. I thought Jack and I were very cozy in our shelter from the cold.

Maybe the men missed their families. Sometimes I would hear them talking in the radio room and they seemed happier when they came out. Jules Madey, a teenager in New Jersey, could patch the calls through to relatives. He stayed up late into the night to help out the men. I bet Jules, being a young guy like me, admired the men and what they were trying to do here.

Men usually settled down for an evening of listening to records, playing cards and writing letters. Maybe the men were writing about life here and maybe they were writing about me! I laid down in my most dignified pose and studied each man with an intelligent look on my face.

Doc Taylor avoided eye contact with me. If he had looked my way I would have taken it as an invitation to play tug of war. I had yanked one of his sweater sleeves to twice its original length, after weeks of seeing who was the strongest. Sometimes he teased me with a tuning fork which vibrated when I hit it. The vibrations drove me nuts!

Bob Benson liked to play with me. One time I nicked his hand with one of my sharp teeth. Doc fixed the cut with some iodine. Arlo would wrestle with me and try to knock my front feet out from under me. I enjoyed this because my cousin used to play the same way.

One evening, Bob, Arlo, Herb and John Guerrero built a fire outdoors. They put some funny looking tubes of meat on sticks and roasted them. I circled the scene carefully because I had never seen a roaring fire. The meat smelled good but I wasn't getting near the snapping logs surrounded by dancing, hissing flames. After they ate the meat, the men ate ice cream on a stick. It was frozen so hard they had to hold it close to the fire to soften it. While I patiently waited for a share, I noticed that Herb was eating the stick. Must be that the ice cream was just as hard as the stick and he didn't know which was which. I like chewing on sticks, two by fours, and packing cardboard. It felt good to rip apart something with my growing teeth.

"Who's the lucky fellow tonight?" asked Ken Waldron. He was referring to the sixteen loads of snow that needed to be brought to the hopper for the snow melter.

"I'm the fellow but I wouldn't call me lucky," Earl Johnson replied. The job was demanding and necessary. The station used over 200 gallons of water each day. Each man was allowed a weekly shower. The galley or kitchen used the most water. It had two 300-gallon tanks that were filled using a pipe from the storage tank in the garage.

"I'm sorry I use so much water," Chet started to apologize. "If the station wasn't at 9200 feet elevation, water would boil at 212 degrees. However my pots boil at 170 degrees and it's hard to thoroughly cook meat. I use the pressure cookers for a lot of dishes. Of course, washing pots and pans is a necessity."

Radioman William McPherson was kept busy. On some days, there were many ham radio transmissions to and from the station. Forty-eight ham radio operators in the States made it possible for the crew to talk with friends and family. Phone patches were arranged so that the men could talk with relatives. News of the Soviet Sputnik satellite's successful launch was received, and the men tried to locate the satellite in its orbit. Dr. Siple was able to deliver a speech via the radio patches and Chet won a Gin Rummy Tournament over the air waves. Contacts with the world outside of the continent helped the men to feel less isolated.

Chapter 5   Everyone Stays Busy at the Pole

I was dreaming of meaty steak bones and Chet's homemade bread. It was being piled in my dog dish, when I woke up to an unusual quietness. I raised my head from the floor and listened with my alert, wolf-like ears, my nose twitching. I couldn't hear any noise from the direction of the generators. Suddenly two men scrambled down the hall pulling on heavy parkas.

When we arrived here, the Seabees were warned about the importance of the generators.

"Diesel-run generators are the heartbeat of this station," Ken Waldron had explained to the men. "If anyone hears even a hiccup from the generators, alert us so we can fix the problem. We have three generators. One was damaged when it was air-dropped from the plane. We don't have a lot of faith in that piece of machinery!"

Jack pulled his lanky body out of bed and listened to sounds of wrenches and raised voices that were encouraging a generator to start. After a few minutes, I heard a hum and the hall lights flickered and started to glow.

"Bravo, that was a weird way to start the day, wasn't it?" Dr. Siple said as he ran his hand from my furry neck to my wagging tail. Paul was a large man and it was an effort for him to get dressed and pry himself out of the small room which housed his cot and all his belongings.

Most of the men were up and seated at the mess hall tables with steaming cups of coffee when we arrived. Chet didn't need electricity to cook because his old stove, made in the 1890s, was heated with fuel. He was flipping pancakes.

"What! No steaks this morning?" my brain asked as I regarded the men who were listening to Jack listing jobs that needed to get done.

"We need the help of everyone to button up this place before the long winter. Dr. Siple will be digging in the tunnel so if anyone has extra time, take turns with him. Only two can dig at one time," Jack concluded.

If Jack helped Paul in the tunnel, I would explore by myself. The tunnel was too cold and scary. I could wait and see if Herb was inflating a weather balloon. He mixed lye and aluminum chips together to produce hydrogen gas which filled the balloon. There would be a transmitter hitched to the balloon that would tell the weather guys about the atmosphere above the station.

Herb Henson inflating a weather balloon. Courtesy of the National Science Foundation.

I remember the first time that a weather balloon was sent into the sky. All the men were looking up at the ascending balloon. I thought the men looked like a pack of dogs getting ready to howl at the moon. They did give a cheer to the meteorologists for a successful launch.

Wind shields had to be added to the tower where the air balloons were released. It was a process, making hydrogen gas and filling the balloon, but releasing the balloon, in strong winds, was more difficult. The sensitive data recorder and transmitter dangled from the bottom of the balloon and Ed Flowers and the other meteorologists didn't want the box to get slammed against the shed. To prevent the winds from blowing the balloon sideways, flaps for the roof were built. That solved one problem.

A second problem arose. When the hydrogen gas was produced from the hot reaction between aluminum chips and lye and water, the steam produced from the chemical reaction rose into the balloon and weighed it down. Floyd Johnson figured out how to make a steam condenser between the gas reaction chamber and the balloon. The steam turned back to water and was drained away while the hydrogen rose into the balloon.

Sometimes the guys found that the neoprene balloons had tiny holes or weak spots that caused problems during inflation. Problem number three was fixed by rubbing diesel oil over the balloon. We later heard that other stations used hot water to toughen up the balloons. The balloons had to be strong enough to rise to 90,000 feet after being launched through the strong Antarctic winds.

Ed Flowers was on hand to see two weather balloons launched each day, twelve hours apart, every day of the week. When the weathermen worked outside, their faces turned into frosted faces. This had happened at McMurdo but at the Pole, the cold made even scarier faces. The men would work for as long as they could stand the cold. I would hear their warnings.

"Ed, you'd better get those readings and get inside. Your cheeks are turning white!"

Ed could work outside with his hands uncovered but he couldn't feel the frostbite on his nose. Some guys didn't wipe their noses because it would make them sore. When a long "snotsicle" formed, they would just break it off. When I first saw snotsicles, I thought the men had long fangs and looked like ugly dogs!

I got used to the balloons and soon looked for other interesting things to watch. Talk about having a hotline to Mother Nature. Ed, Floyd, John Guerrero and Herb Hansen kept track of our base weather. Someone had to go outside every three hours to a base 200 feet away to read the thermometers and instruments. To prevent fogging of the glass thermometers, the men had to hold their breath until readings were done. The instruments were so sensitive that any warm breath would have raised the temperature falsely. Anemometers were used to measure wind speeds and direction. Wind was measured thirty feet above the snow and also near the surface. The men recorded humidity, visibility, air pressure and precipitation.

Moose Remington and Cliff Dickey set out stakes in a long line to measure snow fall. They were surprised to find only a half foot of snow accumulated after a few months. A lot of it blew on by. I could have done a study on that because I was built close to the surface. Sometimes it felt like 50,000 ice crystals blew up my nose. This is not a place where you'd want your eyes to water because they would freeze shut. No wonder my relatives buried their noses in their tails. I've never stayed outside long enough to lie down in the donut position and let the snow blow over my fur insulated body.

If my feet got cold, I would roll over onto my back and put my paws in the air to defrost them. I was in this position when we first heard a thunderous roar beneath the snow. All the men stopped working and looked startled. Dr. Siple quickly reassured them that it was not an earthquake, but a snow quake. The layers of hard and soft snows in the polar layers were shifting and it sounded and felt like a freight train under the snow.

"What is a freight train? Am I supposed to know this?" I asked myself as I tried to sniff out the monster that shook the snow under my paws. Sometimes I would be trotting over the snow and I'd hear footsteps behind me. I'd whirl around to see who was chasing me and there would be no one nearby. The men thought this was hilarious. I later heard that because of the atmosphere, the sounds of my trotting lagged behind me and I was hearing myself only a few seconds later.

Talking about sound and vibrations lagging behind the source, after Bob Benson set up the seismometers at the end of the long snow tunnel, he could pick up vibrations from earthquakes far away. One quake was recorded from Siberia. The seismometers were very sensitive to vibrations and static. For a stable surface, Bob had used water to make a frozen base. He shielded three seismometers from stray electric fields with aluminum foil. These sensitive instruments had not arrived in good condition. At one point Bob tried to solder a gold thread smaller than most hairs. Bob's recorder was a 35 mm film recorder.

Bob Benson with the C-3 ionosonde shown on the left, photo by Cliff Dickey. Courtesy of the National Science Foundation.

"Bravo! Let's play fetch!" yelled Bob Benson getting ready to throw a piece of wood. He was one of the younger guys and was getting ready for a lunch break.

"No sir! Un uh! I like the barracks," I howled over my shoulder to Bob as I headed for the door, wanting to be the first in line for lunch.

Later in the warmth of the mess hall, I watched the men as they ate, hoping there would be leftovers. They ate a lot and I was a growing pup who also ate a lot!

"You'll need to take in over 5000 calories a day," Dr. Taylor told the men as he described how to stay warm while working outdoors. "You'll be eating six to eight pounds of food each day."

"Really Doc, you don't need to tell them to clean their plates! That's my job," I thought trying to look hungry. I don't know how many calories I needed. I ate everything that came my way! I didn't work as a sled dog like my buddies who had returned to McMurdo. In fact, Jack hitched me to a sled one day. I sat down, whined and refused to budge. It was embarrassing when the men laughed at me.

Chapter 6   Passing Time

Even though the men had watched all of the movies, they enjoyed reruns. The screen would be set up in the mess hall and the men would perch on the hard chairs or tables so that all had a good view. One night the men were very quiet, hardly breathing. I raised my head and saw one of those mushy, kissy love scenes in the movie. All of a sudden the table that Jack and Tom Osborne were sitting on collapsed. They were sprawled on the floor with a mess of sugar, powdered cream and butter. I jumped in the middle of the mess, thinking this was so much better than a love scene. The men howled with laughter. I barked with delight. The men cleaned up and went to bed happy!

Besides watching movies, playing cards and games, the men took turns giving lectures in the evenings. Dr. Taylor had lots of medical information to share. Ken Waldron talked about his job as an electrician. Cliff Dickey planned the church services on Sunday evenings.

Dr. Siple told about previous expeditions to Antarctica with Admiral Byrd and life in Little America. It was a rough time for sled dogs back then. Many did not survive. Stuart Paine wrote about Byrd's second Antarctic expedition. Paine had a great lead dog named Jack. One day the men noticed that Jack couldn't move his tail. The dog's tail was frozen and the men had to amputate it. Jack survived. The men tried to fit him with a fleece tail but Jack kept ripping it off.

"The clothing on Bryd's first Antarctica expedition was interesting," Paul continued. "Someone had the bright idea that rabbit fur underwear would be warm. It wasn't! It held moisture, wadded up and felt like soggy diapers! The reindeer coats and sleeping bags were warm but started to shed. I would wake up in the night coughing up hair balls. We had to pick multiple deer hairs out of our food," Paul concluded, making a face as he remembered those mouthfuls of hair.

He added that some of the men wore canvas outer wear that did protect against the wind. If someone's got his jacket wet, it froze.

Then it felt like he was wearing a suit of armor. Men had learned to dress in layers since those early times. The materials used for Operation Deep Freeze were safer and more comfortable.

Jack started to tell about Chinook. I loved the dog stories!

"There's a story about Arthur Walden and his famous sled dog, named Chinook, that's interesting. This large, good natured dog was born in Wonalancet, New Hampshire. All of his offspring carried his traits and a new breed of dogs came about. Chinook was an old dog when he and Arthur came to Antarctica in 1929 with Admiral Byrd.

When other sled dogs couldn't handle a heavy load, Arthur would hitch Chinook and his twelve sled mates onto the load and pull the sledge to Little America. Some of those sledges weighed over 3500 pounds. They pulled it 16 miles. On Chinook's twelfth birthday, three dogs challenged Chinook and he lost all three fights. Maybe this hurt Chinook's pride or his will to live. That night Chinook went outside and was never seen again. Arthur Walden was heartbroken when he lost Chinook," Jack recalled as he passed on some of the stories he remembered reading in books about Admiral Byrd's expeditions.

Jack had studied polar history and he wrote a senior thesis, at Dartmouth, about reindeer husbandry. He had spent time with Vilhjalmur Stefansson. This Arctic explorer was the director of Polar Studies at Dartmouth. Stefansson helped to establish the U.S. Army's Cold Regions Research and Laboratory in Hanover, New Hampshire.

"Stefansson had studied the Inuit diet. He was amazed that the Arctic hunters could survive on meat and fish for six to nine months, without eating any carbohydrates," Jack lectured as he looked around the well stocked mess hall. "We really have no reason to complain about our food this year!"

Drawing by Sarah Tuck Gillens.

One afternoon, not too long after learning about Admiral Byrd, Moose Remington was listening to the Armed Forces Radio station. It reported that Admiral Byrd had died and Moose came to tell Paul. Paul was deeply upset by this news. I watched him from the door of Jack's room and could feel his grief. I stayed very quiet and watched the men as they came by to offer their condolences in soft voices. Admiral Byrd had been a good friend and mentor to Paul and had asked Paul to visit him at his home on Brimmer Street in Boston before heading south. Richard Byrd had looked very frail that day and Paul felt he might not see him again. Paul lowered the Pole's flag to half-mast himself on the 12th of March and left it there until the sun set on the 22nd of March.

Rear Admiral Richard E. Byrd. Photo from Wikipedia Internet site.

Lowering the flag at the South Pole, photo by Cliff Dickey. Courtesy of the National Science Foundation.

Chapter 7   Life Was Not Dull

Everyone was excited when the planes arrived. The mail bag was dropped last so that other gear didn't land on it. If the wind caught a parachute before the men had a chance to cut the lines, the wooden supply pallet would take off across the snow like a flying sled. Men would race after it and I enjoyed this. I could outrun the men most of the time because I didn't wear heavy, insulated boots. I learned an important lesson one day when I bit onto a pallet and was dragged. After that happened, I would bark and encourage the men to catch and fetch the goods themselves!

You should have seen the men scramble when the mail bag broke and letters flew everywhere! Several days later I found a sealed envelope and proudly carried it around in my mouth.

Earl Johnson saw me and got a glimpse of the address. "Hey Bravo, that's from my girlfriend! Give it to me!"

I pranced around as if I had received the letter. As I lunged to the right, Earl lunged to the right and then to the left, reaching out to grab the letter. I couldn't understand why Earl was so upset. He should have been happy that I had found his letter. Didn't he know that I would have swapped it for a nice treat? Jack spoiled my fun when he yelled at me to drop it!

"Oh darn. It was fun for a few minutes!" Earls' face was red and he looked like he was sweating even though it was minus twenty degrees.

Pallets weren't the only thing to be pulled by the parachutes. One day, Willie Hough strapped on his skis and grabbed onto the lines of a parachute lying in the snow. He waited for a strong gust of wind, flipped the lines so that the air caught the chute and off he went across the flattened runway. I think Doc Taylor worried about what would happen if Willie hit the

sastrugi or irregular waves of snow. Willie was
warned to stop before he hurt himself.

Willie Hough para-skiing. Pen and Ink by Sarah Tuck Gillens.

Life was not dull here and I enjoyed
checking out what all eighteen men were doing,
especially Chet, the cook. His stove was pretty
low to the floor. It had been propped up onto
timbers so that Chet didn't have to bend over
while cooking. I couldn't see what was cooking
but my nose told me everything that I needed to
know about what was for dinner. Sometimes the
old stove whined and vibrated when it was really
hot. No one could figure out the cause of this. It
set my brain on edge, like a flock of pesky

penguins who chattered all the time. Chet kept the coffee pots hot at all times for the men.

Drawing by Sarah Tuck Gillens. Bravo trying to figure out the humming sound which probably sounded like a tuning fork.

When Chet baked the first cake in the old oven, it was a failure. He tried again, following the recipe for the cake mix exactly, producing another heavy failure.

"Call up the Arthur Godfrey show! Ask his sponsor why these cake mixes don't rise. I did what the box told me to," Chet grumbled whacking the counter with his dish towel. I dove under a table as our radioman, McPherson, wrote down what Chet wanted. Later we heard that Godfrey had talked about the baking problem on his show. A crew was sent up in a plane to 9000 feet altitude and experimented with the cake baking. It was found that more flour was needed or less baking powder if not using a cake mix. Armed with this information Chet baked and frosted wonderful cakes for the rest of our stay. He kindly decided to bake a birthday cake for me when I turned one on August 14!

Chet turned out some great food on the old stove. He fixed corned-beef hash, tasty omelets, corn fritters and blueberry biscuits. He would have to thaw out foods way ahead of when they were needed. All in all, the men seemed happy with the variety and amount of food served.

Chet made birthday cakes for Dr. Taylor, photo by Cliff Dickey .
Courtesy of the National Science Foundation.

On June 22, the men celebrated the South
Pole winter solstice. Chet fixed an enormous
dinner. The mess hall was decorated with
balloons and streamers. Everyone was in a good
mood. All four mess tables were lined up to
make one long table and it was covered with red

parachute material. Earl had made candelabra from pipe fittings. Chet roasted turkeys with dressing made by Paul. My doggy mouth was drooling with anticipation of yummy leftovers! Some of the men wore funny looking hats and they were given funny smelling drinks. Whew! Moose Remington brought out a large bottle. Its cork sounded like gunfire when it came out of the bottle. I dove under the table!

Cliff Dickey photo. Courtesy of the National Science Foundation.

"Let's make some toasts," Paul announced.

"I don't smell any toast," I thought with my tongue hanging out foolishly.

"To the forty-eight states, our country and the President," said Jack.

"To the IGY as it begins on July first," Paul proposed.

"To our families, wives and sweethearts," Jack replied as he raised his glass.

"To Byrd and to Scott, Amundsen and all those who made our presence here possible – to Antarctica," Paul finished with another sip.

I yipped loudly, proposing that everyone should start to eat!

The South Pole Crew – winter of 1957, photo by Cliff Dickey.
Courtesy of the National Science Foundation.

Back row: Cliff Dickey, Dr. Howard Taylor, Earl Johnson, Bob Benson, Dr. Paul Siple, William Johnson. Middle row: Melvin Havener, Herbert Hansen, Thomas Osborne, William McPherson, Arlo Landolt, Chester Segers. Front row: Jack Tuck, Bravo, Ed Remington, John Guerrero, Kenneth Waldron, William Hough, Edward Flowers.

CHAPTER 8   End of Winter

During the darkness of winter, Paul and Jack spent many hours outside looking at the stars. They took lots of measurements. Both argued over how to find the true geographic South Pole. They took angle measurements from different stars with theodolites. They fussed with calculations. I looked into the night sky and saw dark spaces. These were more frightening than the star clusters. I could sense energy out there.

Jack and Paul using a theodolite to site the geographic South Pole. Painting by Sarah Tuck Gillens.

Keeping equipment running was critical to the station. When the first weasel was dropped, it suffered a broken crankcase. It had to be repaired in order to get the first landing party to the Pole. Jack and Dick had set off the eight miles to the new building site. The mechanics waited for the replacement part. When fixed, the weasel was used to smooth the landing strip. It hauled heavy fuel barrels, to be stored in the long outer corridors of the station for easy access during the dark months. Occasionally, the weasel would help out the Caterpillar dozer.

Photo by Cliff Dickey. Courtesy of the National Science Foundation.

One element crucial to our survival was water. Snow was gathered from an area where traffic was prohibited. Parachutes were handy carriers. Snow was loaded into the snow melting device and melted snow was used for all purposes. The men usually had one shower a week. Washing machines and a dryer were available. The men could hang their clothes in front of the generator fans if the dryer was being used. The Navy forgot to supply soap. Fortunately, some of the men brought some.

"Bravo! You are so lucky. All you have to do is lick and slick your hair to get clean. We've grown beards so that we don't use water to shave," Jack told his hefty dog one evening.

Bravo acknowledged the verbal attention with a tail wag and laid out full length on the floor. He was halfway in the bedroom with his head and shoulders in the hallway. This was a great position. From here Bravo knew if anyone opened a can of peanuts. No one could figure out if it was the scent of the peanuts or the sound of the lid but Bravo would soon appear.

September came as did the really cold temperatures. On the eleventh, the temperature was -99.7 degrees. The men were excited and waited for the thermometer to drop to below 100 degrees. Instead the temperature rose and stayed around -90 degrees for several days.

At breakfast on September 18, the meteorologists insisted that a record would be set that day. After all, spring was right around the corner, just five days away!

At 9:00 AM Ed Flowers came to the mess hall and proudly announced," It's at minus one hundred outside!"

"Come on Jack! Let's take a look at the thermograph in the Met shack," Paul said excitedly, grabbing all his outdoor gear.

"OK Bravo. Let's be part of this historical moment!" Jack said pulling on his heavy mitts.

I followed the excited men outside. Every time I exhaled, my breath froze and tinkled as it fell to the snow. I stayed outside while the men crammed themselves into the shack. They watched the needles on the graph as the temperatures from thirty feet below the surface, five feet above and thirty feet above were recorded. The official temperature at five feet was a -100 degrees fahrenheit. Paul pulled Moose aside and asked him to set up a movie camera. Paul warmed a thermometer to zero and the camera recorded the mercury dropping to -100 degree mark. At 9:30 the temperature dropped to -102.1°. Later that morning Paul had a bright idea!

"Jack, let's go for a hike and enjoy the -100 degree weather!" Paul said with an encouraging smile, pulling up the furry hood to his parka.

"Come on Bravo! We're going to the Pole marker. It's only 2400 feet away," Jack said behind plumes of frozen puffs of air.

I set off with them. Paul complained about his boots feeling like frozen chunks of ice. Jack's black beard was quickly turning white with frost. We were about half way when I remembered the story about the sled dog whose frozen tail had been amputated. That did it! I took a flying leap into the air, gave the guys my blessings for their crazy adventure and I ran for the tunnel entrance.

The sun started to light up the horizon and the men spent more time outside. Finally the sun rose for the first time since March. The men recorded the event with cameras and good moods. I raced around chasing my shadow and hopping on other shadows!

The scientists were busy trying to finish their projects. Ed Flowers and his colleagues had recorded lots of information from their weather balloons. They noted that storms came roaring across from the west side of Antarctica and continued across the South Pole to the east side. It was first thought that our air had less carbon dioxide than populated, industrial areas yet Antarctica's air had just as much carbon dioxide or CO2. There were worries about Greenland becoming warmer and now Antarctica's ice cap would be watched carefully as well. At meal times, the crew talked about what they would be doing when they went home. I was wondering what I would be doing with Jack.

Planes started to drop some supplies and then one landed. A few guys pulled their gear out and walked to the mess hall. I sniffed their tracks, suspiciously. They smelled like diesel fuel and Honey Bucket Lane back at McMurdo. Honey Bucket Lane is where the outhouse barrels were stored. I sneezed and decided I preferred the clean tracks around the South Pole.

The new men brought more than their bags. They brought flu and cold germs that our men caught. Jack and Dr. Siple were both sick. Jack's tall frame was wracked with coughs all night. I stayed by his side and nosed his hand when it flopped over the side of his cot. He didn't even get up for breakfast. I knew that someone would let me outside and then I went to the mess hall. When I came in Chet had filled my bowl. I ate quickly and then noticed the men watching me.

"The Navy is going to sell Bravo to the highest bidder when he is shipped back to Rhode Island," one of the new guys was saying.

"That's not fair," Chet said around his stubby cigarette. "Bravo is Jack's dog. That dog is not a piece of equipment. He's been our mascot and friend, clowning around with all the guys."

"Bravo is known as the first dog to winter over at the South Pole. There will be lots of dog food companies planning to bid on him," the newcomer added.

I didn't like the sly looks the men were giving me so I trotted back to Jack's room. I knew that I was safe with Jack. Dr. Siple was up and trying to dress. I'm so glad that dogs don't get people colds. I gave Paul a sympathetic tail wag as he shuffled toward the mess hall.

In November, some of the men had packed their gear and they were anxious to get home for their holidays. I still had no clue when Jack and I were leaving or if we were leaving. Would this be our home now? Jack seemed to be daydreaming when he stroked my full grown, 105-pound, furry body. He didn't seem happy and I wondered if I had been a bad boy.

By the 20th of November, more men had arrived and sleeping space was limited. Jack had packed his bags and I sat by them expectantly. Jack must have been busy with the new men. I was coaxed into the mess hall and was enjoying peace and quiet with Chet for awhile.

When I was released I took off at a run outside, looking for Jack. I could smell his tracks and then the scent ended. I ran to every man, barking and whining my discontent. I couldn't find a clue to Jack's whereabouts. Dr. Siple tried to console me. This is when I knew that Jack had left me.

I moped around after my barking tantrums ended. The guys tried to cheer me up. When I sneaked back to our bedroom, it didn't smell the same. I could get whiffs of Jack but none were fresh. I remembered our last full day together and Jack's conversation.

"Bravo, you've been a good dog at this station. I think you'll like the new crew coming in for the next year," Jack had said as he scratched behind my ear.

I tried to climb into Jack's lap but he pushed me away. Something didn't feel right. He was praising me but not in a happy voice. I whined.

"You are a big boy; in fact you weigh over 100 pounds. Back at McMurdo, you'll have to share Dogheim with the other dogs.

"What? I'm one of the guys! I don't share leftovers or anything with dogs!" Bravo howled mournfully.

"Give yourself a few weeks and you'll forget about me," Jack mumbled, not believing his own words. "I'm planning on doing polar studies in England and I can't take you over there. Besides the Navy says that all of the dogs are U.S.Navy property and you'll be taken care of by their personnel."

Dr. Siple had come out of his ice tunnel for the last time. He had heard some of Jack's conversation.

"Bravo! You are lucky that you weren't here in 1912 with Roald Amundsen or Robert

Falcon Scott. Many dogs died back then from starvation, cold temperatures or overuse. You've had a pretty good year here."

Later I wandered into the mess hall and overheard Bob and Paul discussing me.

"Bravo is having a hard time with this separation," Bob Benson stated to Paul as I sat by my dog bowl refusing to eat.

"Evidently another mascot is coming in with the new crew," Paul said. "Bravo will fly out with me but then he will go back to the States on a ship. He won't be happy in a dog crate, poor guy. I refuse to be part of this. He's really Jack's dog. Maybe there is a way to fix this problem. I will talk to the top brass at Navy headquarters to see if there's anything we can do to get Jack and Bravo together again."

"I'll braid a leash for Bravo," Willi Hough told Les Liptak, who had just flown in with more of the new crew.

When it was time to leave, Les loaded me on the plane, hitching me to some tanks in the back.

"You stay here Bravo. I have to be up front to help the pilot. Hang on buddy! You'll hear the roar of the JATO rockets needed for takeoff," Les said with a pat.

"Excuse me! I'm not baggage! I'm one of the guys," I whined as I frantically fought the loosely made leash. I managed to get myself free as the plane started to move. Rockets were fired and the plane's engines were revved. So was I, as I hurled myself forward and stood with my paws on Les's shoulders to see where we were going. All I saw was sky and a snow covered horizon.

We flew to McMurdo Station and I was put in Dogheim with other dogs. I guess they beat me up because of my attitude. I didn't know how to act with other dogs. My wounds were so bad that I needed stitches. Some of the guys got together and decided that I should stay in the barracks with them. I didn't go near Dogheim again.

Eventually I was loaded onto a ship and settled into a crate for a long trip back to Rhode Island. It was depressing not seeing Jack and the guys so I slept most of the time. Back home, the scientific data collected at the South Pole was being examined. Byrd, Little America V, Wilkes, Ellsworth, the Pole and Hallet Stations would be adding their findings as well as stations all over the globe. Paul Siple said that all the findings would be examined and would emerge in new physical concepts about the earth. What a lot of work had gone into collecting all that data. Many lasting friendships had been made as the men worked together in that cold, barren place.

My heart felt like a chunk of ice as I was returned to kennels at the home base in Davisville, Rhode Island. As my crate was unloaded, I heard a voice and my pulse picked up speed. It was Jack's voice! I trembled all over until my door was opened and Jack grabbed me in a man hug. I licked his face and howled with delight. My long journey was forgotten and I was happy. Jack was delighted but I could see some strain in his face. Later I found out that the Navy was going to auction off all the dogs. Dog food producers wanted me because I was famous. Newspaper articles had been written about me when I went to the pole as a pup. I didn't even like dog food. I preferred people food! Jack talked about articles in the newspapers which claimed that I should be Jack's dog. I agreed!

March arrived and I was taken to Boston with Jack. There was a ceremony at Constitution Hall and many of the men were there. I was led onto the stage with Jack and Dr. Siple.

Was this the big moment when I'd be sold? I tried to duck under a table. Jack lifted me onto a platform. I panted under the strong lights and warmth of the March day. Maybe if I squirmed around no one would want to bid on me. Jack held on to my leash tightly and made me straighten out as Dr. Siple read from a fancy piece of paper.

Jack, Bravo and Dr. Siple. Photo courtesy of Kathleen Tuck Fontaine.

My name was announced and I heard "has received an honorable discharge from the United States Navy," and then everyone was clapping. Jack was grinning and Paul Siple was shaking

Jack's hand. I licked their faces because they looked so happy! Did this mean that I was free to be me and free to be Jack's dog? I gave one mournful howl and then lots of happy yips as everyone clapped again.

S. 3529

IN THE SENATE OF THE UNITED STATES

MARCH 20 (legislative day, MARCH 17), 1958

Mr. THYE introduced the following bill; which was read twice and referred to the Committee on Armed Services

A BILL

To direct the Secretary of the Navy to transfer certain surplus property to Lieutenant Jack Tuck.

1   *Be it enacted by the Senate and House of Representa-*

2 *tives of the United States of America in Congress assembled,*

3 That, notwithstanding any other provision of law, the Secre-

4 tary of the Navy shall transfer, without consideration, all

5 right, title, and interest of the United States to the dog

6 known as "Bravo," a sled dog born in the Antarctic and

7 now located at the United States Naval Construction

8 Battalion Center, Davisville, Rhode Island, to Lieutenant

9 (junior grade) Jack Tuck, United States Navy, the said

10 Lieutenant Jack Tuck having cared for such dog while living

11 at the American south polar base at Antarctica.

III

Honorable Discharge

from the Armed Forces of the United States of America

This is to certify that

BRAVO

was Honorably Discharged from the

United States Navy

on the 27th day of March 1958 This certificate is awarded as a testimonial of Honest and Faithful Service

C. C. KIRKPATRICK

Rear Admiral, USN

Sarah Tuck Gillens with Admiral Byrd loon, February 2010

When invited to paint a life size carved loon for a fund raising auction for the Children's Hospital at Dartmouth, I decided to create *Admiral Byrd*. I painted the loon as a common loon and then added a brass compass, an aviator's hat with fur lining and sunglasses to protect him from Antarctic glare. As I researched Admiral Byrd's explorations, I read about Paul Siple, first Boy Scout to go to Antarctica. Borrowing Siple's book, <u>90° South</u>, about the first winter over at the South Pole, I found John Tuck Jr., who is a distant cousin. Paul's book doesn't tell readers what happened to Bravo after he was returned to McMurdo Station.

My curiosity was piqued. I "Googled" Bravo and found newspaper Lewiston Sun Journal articles telling

about the Navy's plans to auction him to the highest bidder. Then the research came to a dead end with no reports about the auction. I found another distant relative, Kathy Tuck Higgins in Cumberland, Maine and she told me that Jack had passed away in 1984 and that he had a family. I was able to track down his daughter, Kathleen Tuck Fontaine, and had a nice phone conversation with her as well. She was my source of information and photo of Bravo receiving his honorary discharge from the U.S. Navy.

My first reason for writing about Bravo was to relate a story about a pup born in Antarctica who became known as the first dog to winter over at South Pole Station in 1956-57. After I researched the Antarctic's explorations and subsequent building projects, I gave talks to elementary children about Admiral Byrd and Paul Siple. Most school children had no idea who they were or what they had accomplished. They were thrilled to hear about penguins though!

Then along came Bravo. I found photos of him with "Jack" Tuck and the other seventeen men who stayed at the South Pole for the International Geophysical Year 1957. The planning that went into building stations in Antarctica, the diligent scientific research that was started and the cooperation of Navy Seabees and scientific personnel to ensure surviving a winter at the pole was impressive. I wanted Bravo to tell the story because young folks could identify with his young life's experiences at this remote place. Bravo wanted to go with Jack on this adventure. Bravo's long plane ride left him on a white plain much like a desert with no landmarks. When Jack and Paul worked outside in frigid temperatures, Bravo followed along. Bravo saw the station being built. His puppy antics entertained the men during the long winter dark hours. Bravo shared meals and slept in Jack's room. It must have been difficult to follow the Navy's orders and leave Bravo at the pole when Jack left. I'm sure that Bravo had a difficult time after the separation!

After the ceremony in Boston where Bravo received his honorary discharge and VID – Very Important Dog award from Rear Admiral C. C. Kirkpatrick, Bravo went to the Siple's home in Virginia. Jack went back to school for his masters degree and later went to Cambridge, England to do polar studies.

More about the science and scientists:

Many well known scientists were asked to commit eighteen months to stay in Antarctica for the International Geophysical Year. Most did not want to be away from their jobs for that long of a time. This created openings for younger scientists and college students. The participants were schooled in their field and taught how to survive in arctic weather. Famous explorers like Finn Ronne and Laurence Gould gave lectures about what they had learned in Antarctica. Dr. Siple had already been to Antarctica four times and his participation was critical. After wintering over, the participants went on to give lectures about their experiences, study and teach in their field of expertise and some returned to Antarctica. Jack went back to Antarctica several times, once to measure glacial movements. Paul worked in Washington, DC where he died in 1968.

Questions and ideas for student studies and exploration:

1. Find out what instruments seismologists use. What was Bob Benson able to measure? Do you think Bob could pick up icebergs calving, glaciers slipping or crevasses opening up in the ice? Why

did Bob set the instruments at the end of a thousand-foot snow tunnel?

2. Glaciology scientists obviously study the movement of glaciers. What other important things do they study? Hint: Glaciologists at Wilkes Station set up a hut fifty-three miles inland from the main station. They drilled ice cores 85 feet below a 116-foot deep pit and when the cores were analyzed, there was a high carbon dioxide concentration in the ice formed during the Industrial Revolution. At Byrd Station, the ice cores showed when the Indonesian volcano, Krakatau, erupted in 1883.

3. Ed Remington, a former World War II pilot, kept track of snow accumulation at the Pole. Ed and Cliff Dickey pounded stakes into the snow surface to measure the snowfall over the winter. The buildings were covered but not his snow grade stakes. Why? He found only six inches of snow accumulated over the winter. That's less than an inch of rain. Were they living in a desert?

4. What is geomagnetism and how was it studied by 129 observatories during the International Geophysical Year? Arlo Landolt studied the auroras and air glow. He used a sky camera that took photos of the sky at minute intervals all winter. Why are the auroras most active at the

Poles? What unusual sights would the scientists have seen in the night skies?

5. Willie Hough studied the ionosphere. He wanted to know if the earth's ionosphere thinned out over the Pole. The ionosphere is the electronically charged region 25-250 miles above the earth and it bounces radio waves back to earth, making long-range communications possible. Willie's 75 foot tower and antenna sent high frequency sound waves up into the atmosphere and when they bounced back to earth, Willie measured them on a graph called an ionogram. If the ionsphere is thin in places, does that mean that more of the sun's radiation hits the earth? What would that do to people?

6. What was the lowest temperature recorded at the Pole that first year? Why was it important to use a resistance thermometer? Ed Flowers, Floyd Johnson, John Guerrero and Herb Hansen kept track of the weather 24/7. Their instruments send readings to the base from 200 feet behind the station. Why so far away? One of the men had to go out to check the instruments every three hours. They had to hold their breath while reading the thermometers. Why? Wind speeds and direction were measured with anemometers. Guess who figured out the wind

chill factor phenomenon. It was first named the Siple Index.

7. Can you find, on Goodle Earth, Mt.Tuck named for Jack and Mt. Waldron, named for Ken Waldron, the electrician? What is different about Mt. Siple and how was it formed?

8. Do you think Bob Benson's seismometers measured the snow depth at the Pole? Would it have been possible to drill and get an ice core 9200 feet down?

9. What projects or experiments would you propose if you were at the South Pole? Would the projects help with living in outer space? Would they be useful in deep ocean exploration?

10. Look up the Antarctic Treaty. How could it be applied to national claims as planets are explored? Could it be applied to the Arctic Circle where there is an abundance of underwater oil?

Interesting websites for those interested in knowing more about The Seabees and Antarctica:

www.seabeesmuseum.com

www.antarcticsun.usap.gov

www.antarctican.org/   --The Antarctican Society webpage which has the Yearbook from the first winter over crew. Look under the heading "Pack Ice".

www.explorers.org

www.youTube videos:

C-130 operation with JATOS in Antartic (Spelled incorrectly on YouTube)   29 seconds

Last Flight from the South Pole 6.03 minutes

Mega-Structures – South Pole Station – Documentary - last three years of building new station   43 minutes

Aurora Timelapse South Pole Winter 2011   - awesome aurora australis - 3 minutes

South Pole International Film Festival 2011 – "Goodbye" - there are shots of the first station built by Richard Bower's crew and Jack Tuck and shots of how it looked as a deserted station(but still stocked with food stores) before it was blown up in 2011 - 11.10 minutes

Operation Deep Freeze 1 (Navy released in 1957) - 22 minutes

Operation Deep Freeze 1 part 2 - 10 minutes

Flight To the South Pole (1968) Operation Deep Freeze – Shows film clips from Byrd's first expedition 1929 and a 1968 plane going to and from the pole with a dangerous landing at McMurdo – 28 minutes

Another interesting website:

www.mnn.com/earth-matters/wilderness-resources/stories/south-pole-first-building-blown-up-after-53-years - Article by John Rand of Cornish Flat, NH describes how the original station was imploded because of its dangerous presence under the snow cap.

RESOURCES CONSULTED

BOOKS AND MAGAZINES:

Belanger, Diane Olson, *Deepfreeze: The United States, the International Geophysical Year, and the Origins of Antarctica's Age of Science,* Boulder, Colorado: University Press of Colorado, 2006.

Dufek, George J., *Operation Deepfreeze,* New York, Harcourt, Brace and Company, 1957.

Herbert, Kari, *Polar Wives: The Remarkable Women behind the World's Most Daring Explorers,* Vancouver: Greystone Books, D&M Publishers Inc., 2012.

Paine, Stuart D., *Footsteps on the Ice: The Antarctic Diaries of Stuart. D. Paine, Second Byrd Expedition,* Columbia, Missouri: University of Missouri Press, 2007.

Siple, Paul A., *90° South: The Story of the American South Pole Conquest,* New York: G. P. Putnam's Sons, 1959.

Siple, Paul A., *We Are Living at the South Pole,* Washington, D.C., The National Geographic Magazine, July 1957.

Siple, Paul A., *Man's First Winter at the South Pole,* Washington, D. C., The National Geographic Magazine, April 1958.

Wilson, Patricia Potter and Leslie, Roger, *Eagle On Ice: Eagle Scout Paul Siple's Antarctic Adventures with Commander Byrd,* New York: Vantage Press.

CPSIA information can be obtained
at www.ICGtesting.com
Printed in the USA
BVXC01n0758010414
349353BV00001B/2